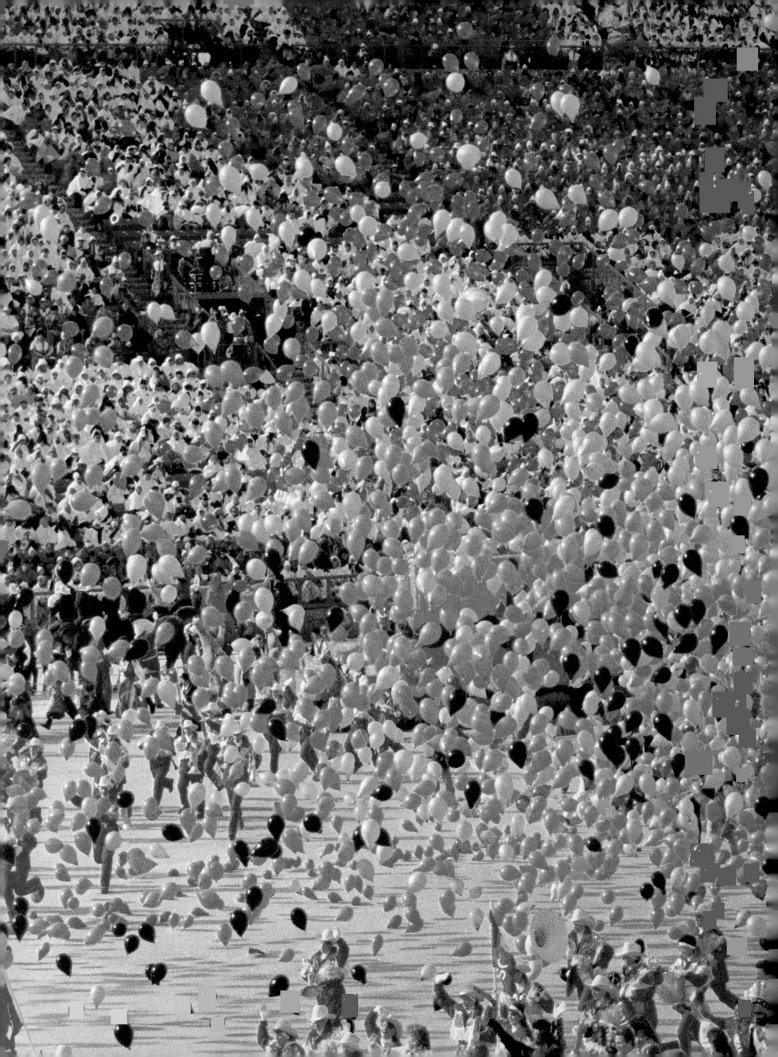

Jill Trenary

THE DAY I SKATED FOR THE GOLD

THE DAY I SKATED FOR THE GOLD

BY **JILL TRENARY** WITH DALE MITCH

PHOTOGRAPHS BY DINO RICCI

SIMON AND SCHUSTER BOOKS FOR YOUNG READERS
PUBLISHED BY SIMON & SCHUSTER INC., NEW YORK

SIMON AND SCHUSTER BOOKS FOR YOUNG READERS
Simon & Schuster Building, Rockefeller Center, 1230 Avenue of the Americas,
New York, New York 10020

Text copyright © 1989 by Jill Trenary. Photographs copyright © 1989 by Dino Ricci.
All rights reserved including the right of reproduction in whole or in part in any form.
SIMON AND SCHUSTER BOOKS FOR YOUNG READERS is a trademark of Simon & Schuster
Manufactured in the United States of America

10 9 8 7 6 5 4 3 2 1   (pbk) 10 9 8 7 6 5 4 3 2 1

Library of Congress Cataloging-in-Publication Data

Trenary, Jill.
Jill Trenary: the day I skated for the gold.
SUMMARY: Photographs and text follow American figure skater Jill Trenary's
final day of competition at the the 1988 Olympic Winter Games, where she placed fourth
out of thirty-one competitors from around the world.
1. Trenary, Jill—Juvenile literature.   2. Skaters—United States—Biography—
Juvenile literature.   3. Winter Olympic Games (15th: 1988: Calgary, Alta.)—Juvenile
literature.   [1. Trenary, Jill.   2. Ice skaters.   3. Winter Olympic Games (15th: 1988:
Calgary, Alta.)]   I. Mitch, Dale.   II. Ricci, Dino, ill.   III. Title.
GV850.T74A3   1989   796.91'092'4—dc19   [B]   89-30554

ISBN 0-671-68315-2

ISBN 0-671-73348-6 (pbk)

To my parents for their support and my friends
who cheered me on during good times and gave me strength in sad times;
also Carlo Fassi, the premier coach who enabled me
to become a national champion;
but this book is dedicated especially to Christa Fassi
who gave me the strength and will to win.
I owe much to the guidance and friendship of this special person. —JT

To Joan Hayward —DM

To my best friend and wife, Sandra —DR

Jill Trenary

THE DAY I SKATED FOR THE GOLD

*I*n 1984, when I was fifteen, I watched the Olympic figure skating competition on television, thrilled when Katarina Witt of East Germany won the gold medal.

It would be like a dream to do that! I thought.

I couldn't have guessed that the next year I would be the United States Junior Ladies Champion. Then in 1987, I became the senior champion; and in 1988, I was named to the new Olympic Team by the U.S. Figure Skating Association.

Along with Debi Thomas and Caryn Kadavy, I was chosen to represent the United States at the Olympic Winter Games in Canada in the ladies' singles competition. I actually would be competing against Katarina Witt and twenty-nine other skaters from around the world. The dream had become real!

I will never forget the Opening Ceremony. It was a cold day, but the pageantry and music helped keep us warm. Fighter jets roared overhead, trailing smoke in the Olympic colors: red, yellow, blue, green, and black. Following exhibitions by cowboys and Indians and dancers, the parade of athletes began, with each nation entering the stadium in alphabetical order.

As the American Team marched into the stadium behind our flag, the crowd roared, and chills went up my spine when the giant Olympic flame was lit and fireworks filled the sky.

But my best memories are of one special day, the last of my three days of competition...

I woke up knowing that this was the day I had waited for so long. The first thing I saw was Lion winking at me. On his eyelid was painted a small mouse.

"Good morning, Lion," I said. "And good morning, Mouse. You can sleep today."

Lion is more than just my favorite stuffed animal, the one I always bring with me to competitions. He is a symbol of the courage and strength that every athlete needs to compete. But like Mouse on his eyelid, inside everyone there is a little mouse who is worried and afraid. The two can live together, and there is a time for each. Today was the day for Lion.

I opened the drapes and looked out on a bright day and snow-covered mountains in the distance. My room in the Olympic Village at the University of Calgary was on the third floor. Below on the street, athletes from different countries were heading to their competitions, a parade of bright team uniforms against the snow.

I shared a small apartment with the other American women figure skaters—four bedrooms, a small kitchen, and living room. I showered quickly and then went to the kitchen for a light breakfast of juice and cereal with some fruit and cheese. We had one late morning practice, and I would eat again after that with my father.

The American men figure skaters were staying in their own apartment across the hall. Brian Boitano, who had won the gold medal a week before, popped in to say good morning and ask how Caryn was feeling.

Caryn Kadavy had become quite sick the day before and had a fever. She was still asleep and we did not wake her. A few of the other team members came by, and after a short chat, Brian dashed off with them to watch the American speed skaters compete.

I went back to my room to begin my morning workout. Lion was waiting for me. I was worried about my friend Caryn. We had gone to the same high school and trained together every day for years. Carlo and Christa Fassi coached us both. They were very well known and had been to many Olympics before, having coached three previous Olympic champions.

I put some soft Neil Diamond music on my tape player and slowly began my exercises. Each one was carefully planned to warm up and stretch the muscles in my back, thighs, calves, and hips, and to strengthen my legs. A skater has to have strong leg muscles to do jumps and spins.

After that, I did deep bends and twists, swinging my arms in big circles. Every athlete has his or her own set of exercises, and does them each day. When I finished my routine, I knew I was in tune with my body and ready for the long day that lay ahead.

After brushing my hair and putting on a little makeup, I picked the clothes to wear for practice and began to pack my bag. I think it is important to look good every day at a competition, especially at practices. If you believe you look good, you will feel better and skate better.

There was a knock on the door and our team leader, Joan Gruber, appeared. "It's almost time to get the bus for practice," she said, efficient as ever. "Do you have everything? Don't forget your identification."

For the past two weeks, Joan had helped plan our schedules, made sure we were on time, and looked after us like a mother. She and our other team leader, Dr. Howard Silby, were always there, just out of the spotlight beyond the television cameras, cheering us on.

I slipped on my red, white, and blue warm-up jacket and pants, the special uniform for the U.S. Olympic Team. It made me feel very special every time I put it on. I picked up my skate bag and started to the door.

Dr. Silby was waiting in the hall. "Good morning, beautiful." He smiled and gave me a little encouraging hug.

When Caryn joined us, I could see that her eyes were red, and she said that she felt a little dizzy. But that was not going to stop her from going to practice. After two days of competition, we were in the top group. We had both worked hard and trained for over twelve years to get there.

The ladies' competition had begun with thirty-one skaters from twenty-three countries. Out of the top six going into the final event tonight, three were Americans. We were the only country to have all of our women skaters in the top group who would skate last.

Debi Thomas was the last one to join us. She was always a little late, but that was Debi. We were very close friends and had sat up the night before talking and laughing together.

"Good morning, all," she said, and nodded. Then linking arms with me, she said, "Let's go."

Those words became my motto for the day.

No one talked much on the bus. We were all starting to focus on the work at hand. I put on my headphones and listened to rock music to raise my spirits and energy level.

The bus pulled into the parking lot of the Saddledome Arena and headed toward the competitors' entrance in the back. Hundreds of people were on the street going to different events.

In front of the arena was a long row of flags of all the nations competing in the Games, hung in alphabetical order. In the blaze of color, I picked out the Stars and Stripes and felt a special pride.

The security guards at the door checked our identification. Music echoed from inside the arena, where another group of skaters was practicing. We took our bags and jackets to the dressing room. Then Debi and I walked out to watch and to wait our turn.

A wide hallway circled the arena under the stands. Off of it, several tunnels led to the rink itself. When we came through the tunnel, I was amazed once again at the size of the arena. Everything was pretty quiet now, but in a few hours it would be full of people and noise.

The seats rose from the barriers at the edge of the ice up out of sight. Giant colored balloons floated from the rafters, almost five stories high.

A lot of people were in the stands watching, but I was used to that. Some were delegates from other countries. Some were skaters I knew. There were judges and officials taking notes, and scores of reporters from the international press. There were also family members of the athletes competing. I knew my own father, mother, brother, and stepmother were out there somewhere.

Debi and I sat next to each other and watched quietly. Debi has a strength about her, and you can feel it just being near her. I felt comfortable and secure with her at my side. We have been friends and rivals for many years. She was the U.S. champion in 1986 and 1988. I was the 1987 champion. The competition on the ice did not weaken our close bond off the ice. Now we tried to support each other as teammates. We each had our own thoughts, and we were both under pressure.

I began to study the ice. I slowly visualized my whole program: checking distances, seeing where each jump or spin would be done that night. The ice surface was larger than the one I trained on in Colorado Springs. I was beginning to feel excited.

We went down through a tunnel into the long hallway, and I began stretching and exercising to warm up again before going onto the ice. Then I hurried to the dressing room to change into my practice clothes while a new layer of ice was being put down. I had just finished lacing up my skates when I heard those words again. Mrs. Gruber stuck her head in the doorway and said, "Okay. Let's go."

My coaches, Carlo and Christa Fassi, were waiting for me. Christa was as bright and cheery as ever. Carlo smiled but looked serious. He is always serious at competitions—and now he also was worried about Caryn.

I started skating slowly around the rink, warming up my leg muscles and getting a feeling for the ice. Every rink is different, and the ice is different in each one. This morning everything felt fine. Bright, lively music came from the giant speakers overhead as six skaters loosened up.

Each skater's music was played after her name was announced. Some people do an entire run-through of their programs. Others only do certain sections.

I never do a complete performance at the last practice. Instead, I work on the hard moves and the jumps and spins. I try to perfect each section yet save my strength and energy.

I skated over to Carlo and Christa and listened to what they had to say. Carlo is a master of the technique of skating. He told me not to rush the jump. I went out and tried it again. It was better. He told me to pull my arm in quicker to help the turns in the air. I tried it again. He was right, as always.

Sandra Bezic, my choreographer, was there, too. She was Canadian, and a skating champion herself. She had also choreographed Brian Boitano's winning program. She reminded me of an arm movement we had worked on and told me to keep my head up and toes pointed.

I went back out and continued to practice the small details. I started a spin and just missed a rut in the ice left by one of the other skaters after a jump takeoff. I would have to watch for such things tonight.

I didn't pay any attention to Debi or Katarina Witt or Elizabeth Manley from Canada or the other skaters. There would be plenty of time for that tonight.

Opposite page, Carlo and Christa Fassi; above, Sandra Bezic

I caught a glimpse of my father in the stands. Sandra's husband, Dino, sat near him. I knew the rest of my family must be nearby. My parents are divorced, and my father has remarried; but we are still a close family. Today would bring us even closer together. Knowing they were all there was important to me.

Each one seems to help in a different way. My mother, who had taken me to so many practices over the years, knows what I am thinking and helps me to relax.

My father makes me laugh. I think he is more nervous when I skate than I am. Sometimes he is so excited he can't sit down at competitions. Then he tells me, "Don't worry so much." But it is hard for either of us not to worry.

My brother, Rick, is the only one who is completely relaxed, and has a wonderful sense of humor. "Even if you slide around on your butt for four minutes, I'll still love you," he told me. "We all will, Jillybean."

It was a good practice. Not perfect. But things had gone all right, and that was fine. I wanted to save the best for tonight. After a discussion with Carlo and Christa, I went to the dressing room to change.

I thought I had seen Caryn leave the ice during the practice. She was lying down in the dressing room and admitted that she felt worse. I could tell she had been crying. She didn't know if she would be able to skate.

I changed quickly, anxious to see my family. I was hungry now, too, but I had promised to do interviews with the television and newspaper reporters from my home state, Minnesota.

My father and Carlo Fassi

It had been almost fifteen years since I first skated on frozen ponds at my grandparents' farm. I learned how to skate by stumbling and falling and getting up and trying again. I had skated many miles from the ponds of Minnetonka, Minnesota, to reach the Olympics in Canada—probably enough miles to go around the world.

The interviews were short. The reporters wanted to know how I felt, how I was skating, and my thoughts on going into the final event tonight as one of the six best female skaters in the world.

When we had finished, Minneapolis television reporter Rob Lear handed me a large box. Inside was a sweatshirt, a hat, and a special card from the world-champion Minnesota Twins baseball team!

"Everyone back home will be watching on television," Rob told me. "We're all pulling for you."

I put on the shirt and hat, thrilled and deeply moved. I didn't think the Twins knew who I was. It was a special moment of the day.

My family was waiting for me. There were kisses and hugs all around. Rick laughed at my new hat, and we all headed out into the sunshine.

I had missed many parties, dances, and dates because I chose to train so hard. But I wouldn't trade any of that for anything in the world, and I wouldn't trade the joy I was feeling right now, even if I could.

The biggest night of my life was only a few hours away.

It was bigger than any party or dance I had ever missed, and I wanted the day to last forever.

While the rest of the family went off to shop and to see other athletes from Minnesota, my father and I went back to the motel where he was staying.

I was starving, and we had a big lunch. I ordered my favorite, spaghetti. On competition days, I always eat spaghetti.

After lunch, we went to my father's room and played gin rummy. I didn't want to think about skating, and I didn't want to start getting ready too early. Besides, gin rummy is one of the few games I can beat my father at sometimes. Today was one of those rare days when I won. I took it as a good omen.

We talked a little while longer. Then it was time to head back to my own room.

The Olympic Village was full of activity, with athletes from all nations mingling and talking. I heard conversations in at least ten or twelve different languages as I strolled past the shops and cafeteria. I saw uniforms from Switzerland, Russia, Sweden, Finland, East Germany, France, Japan, England, Canada, West Germany, Italy, Denmark, and other countries. The world had come to Calgary.

I was wearing my USA uniform and the Minnesota Twins hat. It capped my good spirits.

When I got to my room, Lion was waiting. Mouse was still asleep. I turned on the television to watch some of the other events that were being held—hockey, skiing, and speed skating.

Though I still had a lot to do, I had allowed enough time so that I would not feel rushed. Although I knew it wasn't, I told myself to act like it was just another day, just another competition. Forget it was the Olympics.

I got my skates and sat down in front of the television. While I watched the skiing, I took cotton balls and alcohol and rubbed away the spots on each boot. Then I carefully applied a fresh coat of white polish, making it smooth and even. After it dried, I applied another coat of white polish and put the finishing touches on the boots by coating the soles and heels with black polish to waterproof them.

I put in new laces, taking time to make them straight and even. The last thing anyone in a competition needs is a broken shoelace. There. The skates were ready.

I took a long shower. When I came out of the bathroom, I saw Dr. Silby and Joan Gruber talking softly in the living room. Caryn was running a high fever. She had worked so hard, and now she might have to withdraw. Her Olympic dream was turning into a nightmare.

Back in my room, I put on my headset and listened to the music for my skating program. I closed my eyes as the music played and began to see each movement I would make on the ice.

I started the tape again and began moving around the room. I traced each step of my routine. In my mind's eye, I was seeing it as I would perform it in a few hours. I saw each step, jump, and spin from start to finish. I also tried to imagine the audience, the television lights, the cameras—everything just as it would be.

I checked the time and started final preparations. First, I turned on the curling iron and set my hair. Since I wear it short, I didn't need much time. But today I wanted everything to be perfect.

Makeup was next. Because of all the bright lights, I needed more eye shadow, blush, and lipstick. I looked in the mirror when I was finished. So far, so good. Time was flying.

I packed my skate bag, then opened the closet and took down the beautiful red dress I had been saving for tonight. It was new. It glittered in the fading daylight. The tiny sequins, rhinestones, and small crystal beads sparkled.

I could feel an excitement starting to build as I put it in a garment bag. I slipped on my USA uniform, and I was ready. Lion smiled broadly.

"Time for you to go to work," I told him. I clenched my fists and opened the door.

The rest of the American Team was waiting in the hall. There were high-five's and wishes of good luck all around. Debi, Mrs. Gruber, Dr. Silby, and I headed for the bus. Caryn was not with us. She was too ill to skate and had withdrawn. Now it was only Debi and me representing the United States.

Debi looked at me and grinned. "Don't just stand there. Let's go!" she said.

As we left the Olympic Village, the bus passed McMahon Stadium where the Opening Ceremony had been held. Rising high into the air, the Olympic Torch burned brightly against the night sky. Never had it meant as much to me as it did now.

I closed my eyes to freeze the memory, taking a mental picture. It is a picture I have looked at many times since then and can still see today.

The city was ablaze with lights. The streets were crowded with people. It seemed as though all Calgary had come to a stop for the Games.

Christmas lights had been left up throughout the city. Houses and store windows twinkled brightly. All of the trees surrounding the arena were decorated with tiny white lights, glistening like stars.

Listening to my headset during the bus ride, I thought, *The way it looks outside, I should be listening to Christmas music.*

The competition was under way when we arrived. We had not wanted to arrive too early and have a long wait. As usual, our credentials were checked at the door. I could hear music and applause coming from the arena. After hanging up my costume and jacket in the crowded dressing room, I headed down one of the tunnels leading to the ice. I wanted to see what was happening and how things looked.

I parted the blue curtains and was almost blinded by the television lights. I caught my breath. The audience seemed even bigger than I remembered. As far as I could see across the arena and up into the rafters, every seat was filled. There were over 20,000 people in the Saddledome to watch us skate! I suddenly felt very small at the edge of the ice.

Dick Button, left, and Peggy Fleming

I had come out of the tunnel next to the ABC broadcast area. Dick Button and Peggy Fleming, both Olympic champions, watched intently as they commented. They noticed me and waved. Peggy put her hands together in a gesture of good luck. I tried to smile back. She knew exactly what I was feeling.

There were seven television cameras around the rink. On one side, I could see rows of announcers from over twenty countries. They were speaking into microphones, in their own languages, as the television signal was beamed by satellite around the world.

The corners of the rink were lined with photographers from the international press. The sound of their cameras clicking as each skater passed was like a hundred crickets chirping.

I was suddenly aware of how warm it was in the arena with all the people and lights. I took a deep breath, turned, and walked back through the tunnel to the long hall under the stands. A few skaters were in the athletes' lounge, watching the competition on television. I found a quiet corner and started my final warm-up exercises. Bend, stretch, reach, twist, turn...My body and mind were getting ready.

Not far away I saw Debi starting her exercises, and farther down the hall, Katarina Witt and Elizabeth Manley. Each in our own way began to enter a world of focus and concentration.

Carlo and Christa appeared and we talked a moment. Carlo wanted to be sure I was ready and repeated what great confidence he had in me. It was time to start getting dressed, so Christa and I went to the dressing room.

As I pulled on my hose, my fingers brushed against the deep scar on my left leg. Less than three years ago another skater and I had collided during practice. The sharp blade of her skate pierced my leg, cutting muscles and veins. No one thought I would ever skate again. The Lion in me proved them wrong, for here I was.

Christa helped zip the back of my dress. She turned me around and told me how beautiful it looked and said to try to relax and concentrate. Then she left me alone to touch up my hair and makeup for the last time.

I looked around and it seemed as if everyone was doing the same thing at the same time. The dressing room was overcrowded, and the only mirror was in the bathroom. In the dim light, we all tried as much as possible to look our best.

Katarina stood next to me. Our eyes met in the mirror. For an instant, I thought I saw a look of fear, but she tried to smile. I could almost feel an electricity in the room, but for me it was not fear so much as it was excitement. I couldn't stand still. I can never sit or stand still the last minutes before a competition, and tonight was no exception.

I went out into the hall, paced, and then did some more warm-up exercises. I loosened my shoulders and arms and back, then practiced some movements from my program.

I looked down the hall and smiled. The rest of the skaters were doing the same thing. We did look a little silly in our elegant skating dresses and sneakers. But that is how it is.

A skater is like Cinderella. For four minutes on the ice, she can be a princess. Off the ice, it's unglamorous hard work and concentration. The audience only sees Cinderella.

The backstage television cameras started following each one of us. I tried to ignore them and hold my focus. I felt a long way from Minnesota and my first audience of a few curious cows.

Sandra arrived and I chatted for a few minutes with her and the Fassis. Then Sandra said something that made me think she'd read my mind. "Remember to feel and be the princess in the slow section."

There were only a few skaters left to perform before our group. I went to the dressing room to put on my skates. It may be a superstition, but I always put on my left skate first. After I am sure it feels comfortable, I put on the right one. I let my feet warm up the boots before I lace them.

I found myself sitting next to Elizabeth Manley. She was also tying her skates. Debi sat across from me. She looked at me and winked, then leaned her head against the wall. Her eyes closed and her eyebrows narrowed. She almost looked mad, but I knew it was fierce determination that was building in her.

Katarina Witt sat in the corner next to her coach eating chocolate. I had never seen anyone eat right before competing. Kira Ivanova of Russia, the other skater in the final group, sat against the end wall expressionless, trying not to show how she felt.

We all waited. *Focus, focus, concentrate,* I told myself as other skaters who had finished came in and out of the dressing room. It was almost time.

The door opened and the monitor led us down the hall. Television cameras followed us into the tunnel—five skaters from four countries exchanging good-luck wishes. We all stood huddled at the edge of the ice next to our coaches.

Elizabeth Manley, left, and Katarina Witt

Above, Midori Ito; opposite page, Katarina Witt, Elizabeth Manley (facing away) and me

Midori Ito of Japan was on the ice putting on the performance of her life as she landed one triple jump after another. When she finished a perfect routine, the audience burst into loud cheers. Midori was so happy she started to cry.

Because of her low placement in the first two parts of the competition, she could not win a medal. But she had done her very best, and the audience rewarded her with sustained applause as the judges rewarded her with high marks.

Then the barrier door opened. The five of us started to move forward. I took a deep breath and stepped onto the ice.

As we circled the rink in our final warm up, getting a feeling for the ice, our names were announced. Each name was met with applause. We were the final group, the best ladies' single skaters in the world. The medals would be decided here, and this is what the audience had come to see.

When it was announced that Caryn had withdrawn, the audience voiced its disappointment.

Carlo suggested I practice a couple of my jumps. First I did the double Axel. I circled the rink for speed and picked a spot. The

Axel is the only jump in which a skater takes off while going forward. I bent my left knee with my arms stretched backward. In a single movement I brought my arms forward and my right leg close to my body, thrusting myself into the air. I pulled my arms in tight and crossed my ankles for speed, turning two and one-half revolutions. I kicked my right leg back and landed firmly, gliding in a small arc. I circled the rink again and did the triple flip jump, which would be the first one in my program. Both felt good. I talked to Carlo again, and he suggested I practice a spin.

I was feeling confident and strong but a little too hot. I took a sip of water and wiped my forehead with a tissue. I circled the rink again, skating backward, preparing for my hardest combination of two jumps—one after the other without a step in between. It went well.

I was the first person in our group to skate, and the excitement was pushing me. I felt rushed. I clenched my fists as I always do to pump myself up and went to my coaches at the barrier, but this time not for more advice.

Everything had been said that could be said. I took another sip of water and told them how hot I felt.

"Relax," Christa said. "Don't hurry."

The announcer's voice boomed. "Skaters, please clear the ice."

I skated back and forth in small circles as the others headed into the tunnel toward the back hallway. I clenched my fists again. The barrier door clanged shut. The judges waited.

There I was, alone on the ice with 20,000 people watching. But millions were also watching on television in Europe and Asia and Australia and places I had never seen.

I skated over to Carlo and Christa. They took my hands. Carlo looked deep into my eyes, firing the determination he knew I had.

"Do it," he said. Then as he squeezed my hands, he repeated louder, "Do it!"

The announcer's voice filled the arena again. "Our next skater, representing the United States of America, is Jill Trenary."

I skated to center ice and took my opening position. The audience cheered. As I looked up, I could see American flags waving. Then suddenly it was completely still.

I wanted another minute to relax, to breathe deeply and be sure

The judges

Lion was there. But the first notes of my music sounded, and I started to skate.

I circled slowly, leading into my first spin. Somewhere in that vast arena my family was watching. I knew my father was nervous enough for both of us. I also knew Rick was pulling for his "Jillybean." In four minutes, it would all be over.

"Okay, Lion, let's go!" I went into my first spin. It felt good. I spun faster and faster with a great feeling of freedom. I started down the ice, preparing for my first jump. The rink looked longer than ever. It was important to the judges that I use the whole skating surface.

I was trying to do that and consequently did not reach the speed I needed for the jump—a triple flip. I bent my left knee and reached back with my right toe. I pushed the toe picks deep into the ice and snapped my legs and arms together. I sprung into the air. The minute I took off, I knew the speed and rotation were not there. Instead of three, I did two revolutions—a double jump—and landed safely.

The audience applauded, but inside I knew I had wanted to start with a triple jump—three revolutions in the air in less than a second. It had been a good, high double jump, anyway.

All right, I thought, *now concentrate and hit everything else on target.*

My next move was a split leap into a different triple jump—a toe loop. I skated forward, gently leaning my weight on my right foot, then quickly turned backward and tapped my left toe into the ice, scooping my arms in and catapulting into the air. I whirled effortlessly. My landing was firm.

I prepared for my next move, the combination jump I had practiced in the afternoon. It was as difficult a move as any skater was going to do that night. Both jumps are done off the edge of the skate without help from the toe picks.

First the Axel—1½ revolutions. It was solid. The edge of the blade bit into the ice, and the wide swing of my leg and arm lifted me into the air for my next move, a triple Salchow jump—three complete revolutions. It was clean and firm, too. Four-and-one-half revolutions in the air in the snap of a finger. I heard a cheer go up from the audience. I smiled so that they would know I was happy, too.

The music changed to a slow tempo. Now was the time to catch my breath, a chance to be graceful without so many athletic jumps. Here I was Cinderella at the ball. I was a princess reaching out to the audience. I glided across the ice into a high double jump and landed lightly.

Joan Gruber (partially hidden), team leader, Christa Fassi and Dr. Howard Silby, assistant team leader

Everything was going well. As I rounded the end of the rink, the cricket-cameras clicked away. I passed the barrier. Carlo and Christa were clapping and encouraging me, along with Sandra, Mrs. Gruber, and Dr. Silby.

The next triple jump went well. A fast layback spin with my head and arms bent as far back as I could reach also felt good. So did the next two jumps. The program was coming to an end.

I approached the final jump as the music swelled. The heat, the excitement, and the hard jumps left me feeling a little tired, but a thrill was building inside me. I vaulted into the air. I changed the jump into a double instead of a triple at the last minute. The music ended with a crash of cymbals, and it was over.

The audience was on its feet as I skated back to center ice to take my bow. American flags were waving. People were cheering. Flowers were thrown onto the ice.

I headed to the exit, tired and fighting to catch my breath. Skating for four minutes is no less tiring than running more than a mile at full speed.

My mind got stuck. All I could think about were the first and last jumps. They were not really mistakes, but I had wanted them to be triple jumps instead of doubles. I might have done better, but it was a good performance, one I could be proud of.

When I stepped off the ice, Carlo and Christa each gave me a hug. We sat and waited for the scores. I had a short television interview with Peggy Fleming as the scores were posted. Everything was happening so fast.

Mrs. Gruber and Dr. Silby were waiting to congratulate me. Behind them was Dale Mitch of the U.S. Figure Skating Association, our Olympic press officer. He handed me an armful of flowers that had been gathered from the ice.

"You were beautiful," Dale said. "Beautiful as a princess." He too, had seen the Cinderella I imagined.

The Fassis walked me back to the dressing room and told me to feel proud. I guess I did.

I had so many confusing feelings. I was happy, still excited, starting to relax, but worried about not doing all I had wanted to do. But it was over, and I had done the best I could.

I put the flowers in the dressing room and quickly took off my skates. I wiped the blades dry and put on rubber guards to protect the sharp edges. Then I hurried to see the rest of the competition.

When I got to the crowded athletes' lounge, everyone was gathered in front of the giant television screen. I took a can of soda from the refrigerator and joined the group. I accepted congratulations, then watched the others skate. I sent out all my hopes and prayers to Debi.

Katarina and Debi were both skating to music from the opera *Carmen*. Each one interpreted it differently. Katarina chose the scene from the opera where the flirting dancer dies at the end. Her routine was filled with the movements of Spanish dance. Debi interpreted the happiness and joy and beauty of Carmen. She showed the power and strength of the woman.

Katarina took to the ice. She began slowly bringing her character of Carmen to life. Her program was not as technically difficult as Debi's would be, but she did it beautifully and without a flaw, so received high marks.

Elizabeth Manley skated next. She is a perky blonde, full of energy, and her music and routine suited her perfectly. As a Canadian skating in her home country, she was a favorite with the audience. Tonight was her night. Each jump and spin and strut electrified the crowd. When she finished, we could hear the applause echoing down the tunnel and the long hall into the lounge.

Debi skated last. She looked more nervous than usual. It is very hard to skate after everyone else has performed. Her first jump

Debi Thomas and her coach, Alex McGowan

would be a combination, the hardest of the night. It would be two triple jumps. She faltered and stumbled. A murmur rippled through the audience. She was going for the gold medal, and there was no room for errors. But Debi is a fighter. She came back with other perfect jumps. Then suddenly, she missed another. She finished to cheers from the audience, but it was not the perfect program she wanted.

Like myself, she had missed the opening jump. I knew what she was feeling. Debi was the only person who had ever beaten Katarina, the reigning champion. But tonight was not her night.

When the scores were posted, we saw that she had fallen behind. The final standings gave the gold medal to Katarina. Elizabeth had the best scores of the night. She placed higher than Katarina or Debi, and had moved from third place to win the coveted silver medal. Debi received the bronze. I was fourth overall.

I embraced Debi before the medal ceremony. She was disappointed she had not done better. I reminded her that she had won a medal for the United States and should be proud. In time she would be.

It was thrilling to see the medals awarded and watch the flags of East Germany, Canada, and the United States raised in the arena.

This had been the final competition. The Games were over. Tomorrow would be the closing ceremony.

By the time I finished changing and saying good-bye to everyone, the arena was almost empty. My family was waiting, and after doing a few quick interviews, I rushed out to them.

My father and everyone else hugged me so hard I thought I would burst. There were tears of joy in my mother's eyes and in mine, too. No one cared about the triple jump that wasn't there. What was there was love.

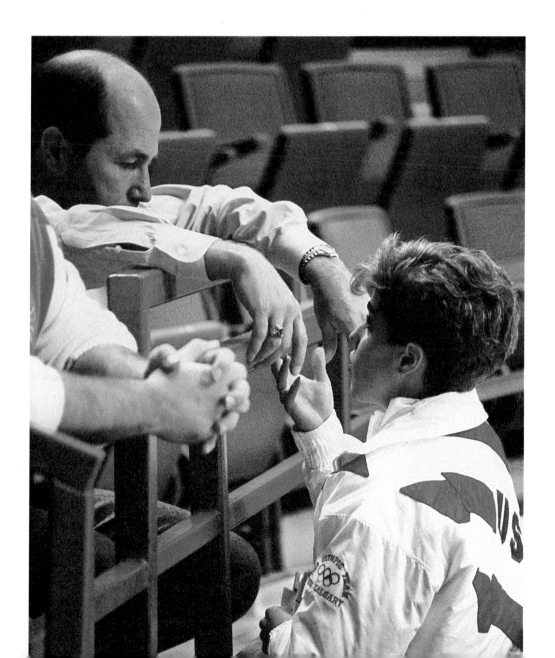

We all locked arms and started out of the arena. I laughed when they told me my father had been so nervous he had stood at the top of the aisle the whole time I skated. Later I would see this and the whole night on a videotape.

We walked out of the arena. The cold night air was cooling and soothing. We went down the street to the car, past the row of flags.

My brother Rick

We all stopped and looked up at the Stars and Stripes blowing in the breeze. I closed my eyes and took another mental picture so I'd remember.

We went to a restaurant. Other friends were there, and it became a celebration. We relived the past two weeks over and over. Everyone had a story to tell about something funny that had happened. I broke my diet and had the gooiest dessert I could find.

By the time I got back to the Olympic Village, it was very late. I had expected everyone to be in bed. But this was the last night of the Olympics, and people were in a party mood. A dance at the disco was just ending. Everyone was trading souvenirs. Lapel pins, flags, tee shirts, hats—one athlete giving a token of his or her country to another. No one wanted the Games to end.

When I reached my apartment, many of the team members were still awake. We crowded into the small living room and talked for a long time. All in all, sixteen figure skaters had come to Calgary to represent the United States. We had won fifty percent of the medals taken by our country. We were all proud and happy and looked forward to the final celebration, the Closing Ceremony the next night.

I didn't realize how tired I was until I went to my room and weariness began to overtake me. I was almost sorry it was over. At the same time, I was relieved. My only regret was that the day had seemed so short. It had gone by too quickly.

I lay down on the bed. Lion was waiting. I pressed him against my cheek. I was already beginning to drift into sleep.

"It was quite a day, wasn't it?" I said to Lion. "You worked very hard. Now we can all sleep."

Down the hall, I faintly could hear a stereo playing the song, "I had the time of my life…"

And just as I fell asleep, I could swear I heard Lion whisper, "We certainly did."

I think back on that day in Calgary often. I look at Lion, who sits in his chair in my room, always ready to travel. On my wall, I see the large certificate I was awarded for placing fourth out of thirty-one competitors.

I did not win a medal. I came close. I feel proud. I feel grateful and very lucky to have been there and been a part of it.

The Olympics are not about medals alone. They are about people and the Olympic spirit that brings together athletes from around the world every four years to meet and compete.

That is what I will always remember the most—the people and the spirit that are the Olympics.

No matter what else I do, I am forever an Olympian. I am most proud of that, and I may have a chance again. Who knows? It is a new dream, and Lion and I are ready.

Biographical Notes

JILL TRENARY was born and raised in Minnesota, where she began skating on the pond at her grandparents' farm. She began taking lessons at age eight and progressed rapidly in the demanding technical sport of figure skating. She moved away from home to study with some of the best professionals. In 1984, she began training with world-famous coaches Carlo and Christa Fassi in Colorado Springs, Colorado. In 1985, she became the United States Junior Ladies Champion, and in 1987 and again in 1989 was crowned the U.S. Senior Ladies Champion. She was chosen to represent the United States in 1988 at the XV Olympic Winter Games in Calgary, Canada.

The final event of the women's figure skating competition was held on February 27, 1988. It was a Saturday and a day Jill will never forget. This is her story.

DALE MITCH is Director of Publications and Public Relations for the U.S. Figure Skating Association, and Editor of *Skating* magazine. He was appointed a member of the U.S. Olympic Committee Delegation to the Calgary Games and served as Press Attache for figure skating. His writings have appeared in numerous publications, including *The Olympian* magazine, *American Skating World, Skating,* Street & Smith's *Olympic Review, Collier's Encyclopedia, The Instructor,* and others.

DINO RICCI first became interested in skaters as photographic subjects through his wife, internationally acclaimed choreographer Sandra Bezic, and has photographed many of her skating colleagues, both professional and amateur. He accompanied his wife to the 1988 Winter Olympics and captured on film its colorful grandeur as well as its private moments.

ACKNOWLEDGMENTS

The photographer would like to thank
William Newton, Toronto, Canada;
Michael Kolb of Midtown Photo, Downsview, Canada;
and Reg Anaka of ABL Photo in Calgary, Canada.

All photographs by Dino Ricci except for
cover photo by DUOMO/David Madison;
pages 40 and 46 by DUOMO/Steven E. Sutton;
pages 47 and 48 by ALLSPORT/Mike Powell;
and pages 50 and 58 by DUOMO/David Madison.

Special thanks to Michael Rosenberg

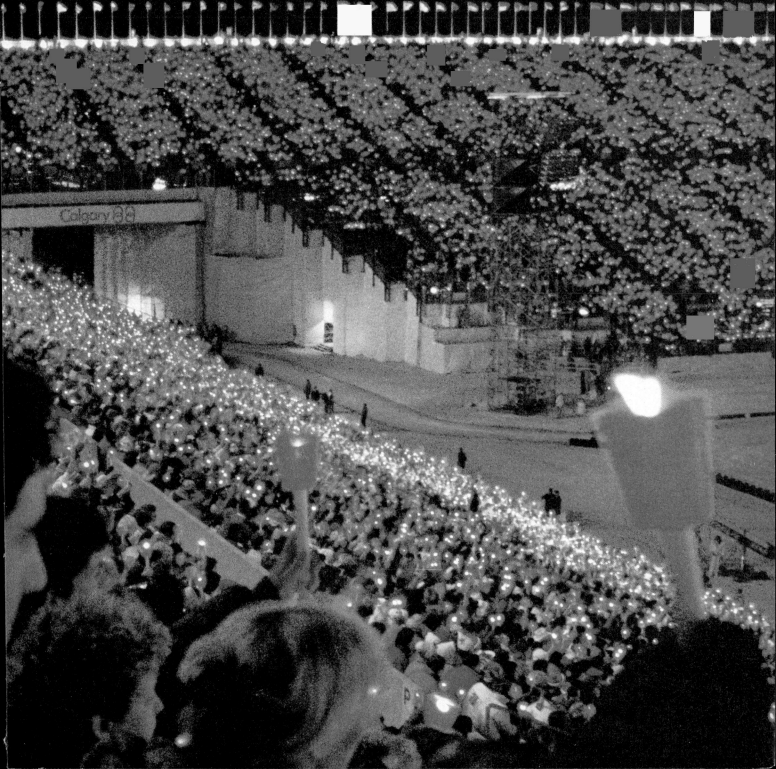